Let's Explore
Peanut Butter!

Jill Colella

Lerner Publications ◆ Minneapolis

Hello Friends,

Everybody eats, even from birth. This is why learning about food is important. Making the right choices about what to eat begins with knowing more about food. Food literacy helps us to be more curious about food and adventurous about what we eat. In short, it helps us discover how delicious the world of food can be.

Doesn't it feel good when your body feels full of energy? Protein foods like peanuts help us move and play. Peanuts pack a ton of energy to fuel our bodies. That's a great reason to eat them!

For more inspiration, ideas, and recipes, visit www.teachkidstocook.com.

Jill

About the Author
Happy cook, reformed picky eater, and long-time classroom teacher, Jill Colella founded both *Ingredient* and *Butternut*, award-winning children's magazines that promote food literacy.

Note: Some people cannot eat peanuts because they have an allergy. Respect people who have allergies by keeping peanuts safely away from them.

Lerner Publications Company
An imprint of Lerner Publishing Group, Inc.
241 First Avenue North
Minneapolis, MN 55401 USA

For reading levels and more information, look up this title at www.lernerbooks.com.

Main body text set in Mikado
Typeface provided by HVD

Library of Congress Cataloging-in-Publication Data
Names: Colella, Jill, author.
Title: Let's explore peanut butter! / Jill Colella.
Description: Minneapolis, MN : Lerner Publications, 2020. | Series: Food field trips | Includes bibliographical references and index. | Audience: Ages 4–8 | Audience: Grades K–1 | Summary: "Introduce young readers to peanuts by showing them what peanut plants look like and how they grow. An easy recipe and a simple craft project invite readers to engage with this longtime favorite ingredient."—Provided by publisher.
Identifiers: LCCN 2019045749 (print) | LCCN 2019045750 (ebook) | ISBN 9781541590335 (library binding) | ISBN 9781728402840 (paperback) | ISBN 9781728400211 (ebook)
Subjects: LCSH: Cooking (Peanut butter) | LCGFT: Cookbooks.
Classification: LCC TX814.5.P38 C65 2020 (print) | LCC TX814.5.P38 (ebook) | DDC 641.6/56596—dc23

LC record available at https://lccn.loc.gov/2019045749
LC ebook record available at https://lccn.loc.gov/2019045750

Manufactured in the United States of America
1 – CG – 7/15/20

SCAN FOR BONUS CONTENT!

Table of Contents

Picture Glossary

dig

flowers

peanuts

pods

shells

ALL ABOUT PEANUTS

Peanuts are small seeds. They grow inside the pods of the peanut plant.

Peanuts are made into peanut butter and peanut oil. They can also go in salads, cookies, and curries.

LET'S COMPARE

Peanuts are known as nuts. But they are actually legumes.

Legumes are plants that grow pods. Peas and beans are also legumes.

How are peanuts, peas, and beans alike? How are they different?

LET'S EXPLORE

Peanuts grow in fields. They grow under the ground in pods.

A peanut plant has many pods. Inside each pod are seeds. These are peanuts!

LET'S VISIT A PEANUT FARM

Farmers plant peanut seeds in long rows. Farmers cover the seeds with soil.

Bushy plants grow up through the soil. The plants need sunshine and water to grow.

What else needs water to grow?

Yellow flowers appear on the plants. Their petals fall off. Then their stems grow down into the soil.

Pods form underground. Peanuts grow inside the pods.

Farmers dig up the plants.
Do you see the pods that
grew underground?

What else can the sun do?

The pods sit in the sun
to dry out.

The pods harden into shells. Crack open a shell to find seeds inside.

How many seeds
do you count?

Most pods have two seeds
inside. But some have more.

17

Farmers send the peanuts to be roasted. Then the peanuts are ground into a creamy spread.

This is peanut butter!

LET'S COOK

Always have an adult present when working in the kitchen!

EASY PEANUT BUTTER

INGREDIENTS

- 1 cup (148 g) unsalted, roasted peanuts (plus more for chunky peanut butter)
- 1 teaspoon peanut oil
- ¼ teaspoon salt

1. Place all the ingredients into a blender.

2. Have an adult help you pulse the blender to break down the peanuts. If necessary, stop the blender and scrape the mixture from the sides of the container using a rubber spatula.

3. Continue blending until the mixture is as creamy as desired.

4. For chunky peanut butter, stir in ½ cup of chopped peanuts after the blending is completed.

5. Store the peanut butter in a tightly sealed container in the refrigerator. Oil may rise to the top. If this occurs, stir before using.

SEE THIS RECIPE IN ACTION!

LET'S MAKE

PEANUT BUTTER BIRD FEEDER

MATERIALS

- wire or paper clips
- pine cone
- large pan
- birdseed (or crushed cereal)
- spoon
- peanut butter
- ribbon or yarn

1. Wrap wire around the core of the pine cone, near the wide end. Make a loop. You'll tie the ribbon here later.

2. Pour birdseed in a pan. Set the pan aside.

3. Use a spoon to cover the pine cone with peanut butter. Be sure to get peanut butter in all the small openings of the pine cone.

4. Roll the coated pine cone in the birdseed. Use your fingers to stick as much birdseed as possible onto the pine cone.

5. Tie the ribbon to the loop in the wire. Then hang the pine cone outside!

Let's Read

Cook, Deanna F. *Cooking Class: 57 Fun Recipes Kids Will Love to Make (and Eat!)*. North Adams, MA: Storey Publishing, 2015.

Georgia Peanut Commission—Peanut Circus Club
http://www.peanutcircusclub.com

Hansen, Grace. *How Is Peanut Butter Made?* Minneapolis: Abdo Kids, 2018.

National Peanut Board—How Peanuts Grow
https://www.nationalpeanutboard.org/peanut-info/how-peanuts-grow.htm

Nelson, Robin. *From Peanut to Peanut Butter*. Minneapolis: Lerner Publications Company, 2013.

Texas Peanut Producers—How Do Peanuts Grow?
http://texaspeanutboard.com/news/576/

Photo Acknowledgments

The images in this book are used with the permission of: © AlasdairJames/iStockphoto, p. 23; © Alfribeiro/iStockphoto, pp. 3 (tractor), 14 (tractor); © anmbph/iStockphoto, pp. 3 (flowers), 12; © avdeev007/iStockphoto, p. 17; © baianliang/iStockphoto, p. 8 (peanut field); © baibaz/iStockphoto, p. 1; © Catto32/iStockphoto, pp. 3 (shelled peanuts), 6; © chas53/iStockphoto, p. 5 (cookies); © chomplearn/iStockphoto, p. 8; © cisilya/iStockphoto, p. 22; © doğuhan toker/iStockphoto, pp. 3 (pods), 9; © EdrZambrano/iStockphoto, p. 5 (girl spreading peanut butter); © Elenathewise/iStockphoto, p. 7 (peas isolated); © fcafotodigital/iStockphoto, pp. 3, 4, 16; © FotografiaBasica/iStockphoto, p. 7 (bowl of black beans); © FuatKose/iStockphoto, p. 7; © hudiemm/iStockphoto, pp. 8 (hand holding peanuts), 11 (peanut leaf with rain droplets); © Image Source/iStockphoto, p. 19; © Jasonfang/iStockphoto, p. 11 (farm field); © Mailson Pignata/iStockphoto, p. 18; © Maryna Iaroshenko/iStockphoto, p. 21; © Photo-Dave/iStockphoto, p. 20; © Singkham/iStockphoto, p. 10; © tashka2000/iStockphoto, p. 5; © Vladimir Mironov/iStockphoto, p. 18 (peanut butter); © wilaiwanphoto/iStockphoto, pp. 13, 14, 15; © y-studio/iStockphoto, p. 11.

Cover Photos: © 4kodiak/iStockphoto (peanut butter on bread); © baibaz/iStockphoto; © Image Source/iStockphoto (boy and dad); © Sanny11/iStockphoto (jar of peanut butter); © studiocasper/iStockphoto (peanuts isolated on white)